NIGERIAN
FOOD PLATING

By *Chef Muse*

Series 1

NIGERIAN

FOOD PLATING

[

This work is ded
you are s

First publication - Nigeria 2022 by:Chef Muse

ISBN:

Printed in Nigeria by Dowins GlobalLink Limited
Written byTahir Muneera (Chef Muse)
Photography by Chef Stone. Yetunde Abass. Chef Muse
Images were created in Red Dish Chronicles Culinary SchoolAbuja.
Designed by Dowins DesignerTeam
Food Plating byTahir Muneera (Chef Muse)

Note for the Reader
This book uses metric measurements. Follow the same units of measurement throughout. All spoon and cup measurements are level: teaspoons (tsp) are assumed to be 5ml, tablespoons (tbsp) are assumed to be 15ml and a cup is assumed to be 250ml. Unless otherwise stated. Habaneros are freshly blended, all root vegetables should be peeled prior to using and milk is assumed to be full fat. Unless otherwise stated.

The times given are an approximate guide only. preparation times differ according to the technique used by different people and the cooking time may also vary from those given.

dowins

Acknoledgement

The pleasure that follows the completion of this book would remain incomplete without a word of gratitude for the people without whose support the achievement would remain a distant dream.

I am eternally grateful to God almighty for his infinite blessings. To Mr and Mrs Santangelo, you both believed in me when I didn't know what it meant to believe in myself and for this I am profoundly grateful. May God reward you abundantly. My sincere gratitude to My Leader Extraordinaire Chef Stone, your dynamism, vision, sincerity, and motivation has deeply inspired me. My heartfelt gratitude to Chef Zee, remember that call? It changed everything, may God bless you richly. For the RDC crew, Maryam, Chef Boxiy, Chef Blade, Chef Denike, Chef D Onnit), Yetunde Abass, TK Williams, Olamide, Chef Tach, Chef Posa, Vivian, Chef Sammy, Happiness. Thank you all for your constant support.

I am extremely grateful to my parents for their invaluable prayers. Dear Onyami, look at me. A special thanks to my friend Chibuzo Namdi-Okagbue for the guidance and to Muyiwa (glass onions), Genesis, Chef Shubby and Asugha Uche I am grateful. To my family and friends, thank you and I love you all.

Contents

Introduction

This is a series featuring different cuisines from all over Nigeria plated in the most exquisite ways that its almost hard to believe they are actually dishes and not raw art. This idea birthed from the need to 'as cliché as it sounds' go outside the box to showcase popular Nigerian food staples in never before seen ways. From pepper soup to Ewa Agoyin and abacha.

This book is a pictorial representation of how I see Nigerian food today and in the nearest of future. During my research before embarking on this project, I was saddened by the way Nigerian meals were represented on the internet. The internet is a place to find any and everything you might have ever imagined unfortunately had Nigerian food in the most mediocre and neglected light. It got me asking questions like;

Why can't Nigerian food be plated in a fine dining style?

Why can't Nigerian meals not even considered fine dining worthy?

Why are we as people not willing to learn about other meals from different tribes?

These questions along with the need to put Nigerian food on the global map kickstarted the urge to put this work out. I spent months creating new ways of showcasing Nigerian meals as well as other exciting never before seen ways to showcase the popular staples. Nigeria is rich in culture and diversity, our food should say this to the world. This book is ready to take you on an ultimate culinary visual experience.

Getting The Most Out Of Food Plating

The dictionary definition of food Presentation is "the art of modifying , processing, arranging or decorating food to enhance its aesthetic appeal". I would say it isthe way of harmonising all five senses into the experience of eating. A wellpresented food would have you spending so much time adoring the piece of art before eating. It harmonises the sense from the sound it makes when the food is being cooked, the texture you get as a result of the technique applied, the beautifulcolours for your eyes because youvisually taste the food before it hits your tongue, the aroma pleasing the nose and the unforgettable taste to match the beauty, HARMONY.

Food plating and presentation is basically youmanipulating the ingredients to get the best out of it. For example, the way heat is being applied to food and the technique used in cooking the food gives a different outcome. Colour adds energy and contrast to your dish. Bright vegetables such as carrots, spinach, red cabbage make a striking difference on a plate. Work with complementary colours and try beautifying salads and meats with banana or Uma (moi moi) leaf or citrus zest. A large plate is always a great idea for a main dish because it gives you more space to work with, please avoid the pressure to completely fillupcheplate, leave some breathing room. Garnishes can add flavour and texture to your finaldish, it shouldn't be an after thought but rather an edible element that ispurposely placed to balance the overalldish.

Free your mind, get creative and use plates from natural materials like wood, stones, clay pots, leaves as wellas unusual bowls and so on. Use tools like precision spoons, squeeze bottles, decorating brushes, slotted spoons, sieves, moulds and most importantly your hands to express yourself on a plate. So open your mind, apply different cooking methods and see how the same ingredient can give you different result. Food plating takes ample time anda lot of patience but it is achievable.

Whenever you want to plate, think ofthe plate as your body, arrange the components ashowyou would dress up,entice the eyes withvisualstimulants, usesauces aspaints and garnishes to enhance both appearance and flavour, then watch how food plating and Presentation become your play ground. Be courageous, be persistent. be focused andexpress the artist in you.

Street Corners

Asun ...The MC with the MSE!

Smoked boneless goat. hot and spicy with sweet undertone from the caramelised pepper mix and onion. It is smokey, it is sizzling, it is juicy, it is tender and ah! Owa mbe!!!

INGREDIENTS	FOR THE FLAT BREAD
2kg goat washed, pat dry.deboned and cut into bite size chunks.	2009 warm water
Minced habaneros as desired	1009 warm milk
1 green bell pepper julienned	1tsp yeast
1 red bell pepper julienned	2509 flour sifted
1 large onions julienned	1tbsp sugar or honey
Seasoning and salt to taste	3 tbsp yogurt
1/ 4 cup palm oil or vegetable oil	Pinch of salt
1 tsp curry powder	1tsp baking powder
1tsp thyme	1tbsp Melted butter or vegetable oil and extra for frying
1 tsp minced ginger	
1tsp minced garlic	**PLATING TOOLS NEEDED** Culinary twine Brown parchment paper

INSTRUCTION	FOR THE FLAT BREAD
1. Place the meat in a large saucepan over medium high heat.	1. In a large bowl. pour the warm water. milk. yeast. sugar or honey. yoghurt. mix to combine and set aside for 5 minutes.
2. Add the curry. thyme. garlic. ginger. pepper. half of the onion. seasoning and salt to taste.	2. In a separate bowl. add the flour. baking powder. salt and mix.
3. Cover and let cook in its own juice till the liquid in it is dry.	3. Pour the liquid ingredients into the dry ingredients and mix vigorously.
4. Start tossing the meat and let it brown nicely, scraping the bottom of the saucepan occasionally.	4. Cover and let sit in a warm place for 30 minutes or until double in size.
5. Reduce the heat. add the palm oil and onion.	5. Heat a nonstick frying pan over a medium low heat. brush it with melted butter or oil.
6. Allow to fry till the onion is soft caramelised.	6. Scoop the mix and spread it evenly on the pan using your hand or brush.
7- Now add enough water to cover the meat.	7- Let it cook for about 2 - 3 mins.brush the top with oil and flip it over to cook on the other side.
8. Cook the meat till tender.	
g. Reduce the heat and let it cook slowly till the liquid is velvety and glossy but not dry.	8. continue till the batter is exhausted.
10. Add the bell peppers. adjust seasoning and serve.	**TO ASSEMBLE** 1. Lay the bread. brush it with butter. fill it up with the Asun.
	2. Wrap it up with the brown parchment paper. using the culinary twine to hold it together.
	3. Serve immediately.

Ewa Agoyin   The street lord!

This battleispersonalbecause beans is one of my favourite food.Hold up!Have you triedsearching this particular dish on the internet? The results aren't even encouraging for anyone who doesn't know anything about this glorious dish to want to give it a try.The funny part isthat when you taste it onceyou willbehooked. Great flavour, amazing textures, the sweet undertone from thecaramelised sauce pairs fantastically with thebuttery texture of the beans. As a beans Lover, my heart crushes every singletime I Look up this dish on the internet andthat's howwe endedup here ire!!!

INGREDIENTS

2 cups honey beans pickedandwashed
1 cup palm oiL
8 dried tatashe soaked overnight
3 dried habaneros soaked overnight
5 driedchillisoakedovernight
4 fresh habanero
2 Large ripetomatoes
1/2 tsp minceginger
3 tbsp blended crayfish
Salt and seasoning to taste
1 medium onion sliced and divided
3tbspbutter
2 fingers not very ripe plantain, cleaned and thinly slicedLengthwise
Vegetable oil for frying

PLATING TOOLS NEEDED
Spoon
Pipping bag

FOR THE PLANTAIN

1. Heat up the vegetable oil in a deep frying pan.
2. Fry the plantain till crisp, drain on paper toweland setaside.

TOASSEMBLE

1. Get a suitable plate, preferably round and flat plate.
2. Use the Spoon to scoop enough of the mashed beans, place it on the plate and carefullyswirlit round.
3. Pour the sauce in a piping bag and carefully pipeit in-between the mashedbeans.
4. Toss the reserved beans with some of the oil from the sauce and arrange nicely on the mashed beans to createacontrast.
5. Take the plantaincrispandarrange it on top.
6. Serve immediately.

INSTRUCTION

1. Place the tatashe, habanero, chilli, fresh habanero, ginger, half of the sliced onion, tomato in foodprocessor and roughly blend andsetaside.
2, Pour enough water in a pot. add the beans, place it over a medium high heat. cover and cook till soft and mushy (use pressure cooker for a faster result).
3, While the beans is cooking prepare the agoyin sauce.
4- Place a medium saucepan over a medium high heat, add the palm oil and heat it up for 3mins.
5- Add the remaining sliced onion and fry till caramelised.

6. Add the roughly blended pepper, reduced heat to Low and fry for about 3ominutes stirring occasionally so it doesn'tburn.
7- Add the crayfish and season to taste and Letfry for another 5-10minutes.
8. At this point you should get a smoother, caramelised but not burnt sauce with agoyin aroma.
9, Adjust seasoning and setaside.
10, When the beans is very soft. season with salt to taste and scoop out 3 tbsp and set aside.
11. Use a masher to mash the beans to a slightly roughand buttery consistency.
12. Add the butter and whip till fluffy, adjust seasoning andset aside.

Suya & Gurasa TheNightKing!

Tenderised grill meat. succulent, spicy with the Nigerian flat bread aka gurasa tossed in grounded kulikuliwith peanut oil. I wouldn't say much but. oooommmmmmmooooooo!

INGREDIENTS FOR THE CHICKEN SUVA	FOR THE GURASA
1.5 kg chicken wings 4 tbsp grounded kulikuli 1tbspcayenne pepper 1tbspyaji 1tbspsmoked paprika 1tbspgarlic powder 1tbspginger powder 1tbsponionpowder 11/2tspground cloves Salt and seasoning to taste 1/2 cup groundnut oil Wooden skewers soaked in water for at least30minuter 2 hard ripe tomatoes washed and cut into wedges 1smallonion cleaned andcut intowedges 3 - 4lettuceleaves washed and shredded	2 cupsflour sifted 1 cup warm water 1tsp active instant yeast 11/2tbspyoghurt Pinch of salt 1tbspsugarorhoney Vegetable oil for brushing **PLATING TOOLS NEEDED** Foilpaper Brownparchment paper

INSTRUCTION

1. Mix all the spices together for the suya in a bowl.
2. Preheat the oven at180 degrees Celsius.
3. sprinkle the spices evenly over the chicken wings and let marinate for at least 30 minutes.
4, Meanwhile combine all the ingredients for gurasa together in a large bowl and mix vigorously.
5. Cover with plastic wrap and let it sit in a warm place for 30 - 45minutes
6. Turn it over a lightly floured surface and knead.
7- Cut into5 equalballsand rollit flat. leave it to rest for 5minutes.
8. Arrange the chicken wings in an oven rack, brush withtheoil.
9, Place it in the middle of the oven then place an oven tray underneath the rack for drippings.

10. Grill for 30 minutes, flipping and brushing every10 minutes.
11. Place a nonstick pan over a medium high heat.
12. Brush the pan with oil and place the bread on top.
13. Cook on each side for at least 2 - 3 minutes
14, Serve with thesuya.

TOASSEMBLE

1. Get the foil paper and parchment paper just enough to carry the suya and squeeze the edges.
2. Cutthe gurasa intoquarters.
3. Layer it on top of each other, place the wings by the side.
4, Arrange the lettuce, tomatoes and onion.
5, Dust it with yaji and drizzle some of the drippings on it.
6. Serve immediately.

Ugba & Roasted Yam

...Popular Jingo!

Another popular street foodsaving lives but not beingpresented well. 0 wrong sha!

INGREDIENTS	PLATING TOOLS NEEDED
1medium tuber of yam. washedwith skinon. slicedandsoaked insaltwater for at least 30 minutes 2 thick ponmo (cow skin) cleaned and cut intobitesize 1tbspgrounded crayfish 1 cup ugba (oilbean) cleaned 5habaneros or as desired roughly blended I medium onion sliced 1/2 cup palm oil Few slices of uziza and utazi leaves for garnish 1/2 tsp ground ehuru Salt and seasoning to taste 1cupwater	Ring cutter Spoon

INSTRUCTION

1. Set the charcoaltillitsburning bright.
2. Use the ring cutter to cut the yam forming a crescent.
3. Wrap the yam in foilpaper and place on top of the coal (this helps it to cook from the inside).
4. Lettheyamroast for 10 minutes.
5. Remove the yam from the foil.scrape gently and put it back on the hot coalfor another 3-5 minutes to char nicely.
6. Remove fromthe fireandsetaside.
7- Place a medium saucepan over medium high heat.
8. Place the ponmo. the water, season to taste andcook tilltender.
g. By thistimethewater isalmost dry.
10. Add the pepper. onion,palm oilandcook for another3 minutes.
11. Add the crayfish, ehuru, ugba and toss nicely.
12. Adjust seasoning to taste and garnish with theslicedleaves.

TO ASSEMBLE

1. Get a niceplate.
2. Place one slice of yam flaton the plate.
3. Mount the secondsliceon top.
4. Use your spoon to scoop the ugba and arrange it nicely insidethe crescent.
5. Drizzle oil around it and sprinklesome of the sliced leaves on it.
6. Serveimmediately.

Abacha   .weintheeast!

African salad as it is popularly called. Made from cassava flakes. with onion. garden eggs. and mackerel. The emulsified sauce is made with fantastic spices and the gluten from the cow skin after being cooked down. Can be great as an appetiser or hearty as a main meal. A trial will convince you kaa puo!

INGREDIENTS	PLATING TOOLS NEEDED
3 cups cassava shavings (abacha) cleaned and soaked in water for 10 minutes 1 cup ugba (oilbean) cleaned 1/2 cup palm oil 1 mackerel gutted. head off. fillet and cleaned 1 tsp edible potash dissolved in 1/4 cup water 2009 stockfish flakes cleaned 3 habanero or as desired 1 small red onion julienned 3 medium garden egg julienned 1 tbsp ground crayfish 1 tsp ground ehuru (calabash nutmeg) Salt and seasoning to taste Vegetable oil for frying 5 utazi leaves cleaned and sliced	Spoon **TO ASSEMBLE** 1. Get a nice flat plate. 2. Use your spoon to scoop the sauce. 3. Place on a plate and create a "c" in three places overlapping each other. 4. Place the fish just by it. 5. Scoop the mixed abacha and arrange it next to the fish. 6. Garnish the abacha with some of the garden egg. onion and utazi leaf. 7. Serve immediately.

INSTRUCTION

1. Put the stock fish flakes in a medium saucepan over a medium high heat.
2. Season to taste and add enough water at least 2 cups.
3. Cover and cook for 30 minutes or till tender and set aside.
4. Season the fish to taste and let marinate for about 15 minutes.
5. Meanwhile strain the abacha and let it drain.
6. Heat the vegetable oil in a deep frying pan.
7- Deep fry the fish till golden brown and cooked through. drain on paper towel and set aside.
8. Blend the pepper and half of the onion till smooth.
g. Pour the palm oil in a medium saucepan over low heat.
10. Add the onion and pepper to cook slowly and stir occasionally.
11. Add the potash liquid. mix vigorously to incorporate nicely.
12. Add the crayfish. ehuru, salt and seasoning to taste. mix well to combine.
13. Scoop out a few of the sauce and set aside.
14. Add the abacha. stock fish. ugba. the julienned garden egg and reserve some for garnish.
15. Turn off the heat and toss to combine.
16. Adjust seasoning to taste and serve.

STREET CORNERS

Kosai/Akara ...the breakfast king!

Enjoyed by millions everyday, most popular street food, can be eaten on its own or paired with pap, custard. oat and bread. I promise you it is enjoyable whichever way you decide to eat it.

INGREDIENTS

4 cup beans. skin peeled and soaked in water for at least 30 minutes
4 habanero or as desired cleaned
3 tatashe cleaned and deseeded
1 medium onion cleaned and divided
3 large eggs
Salt to taste
Vegetable oil for frying
Yaji for serving

Bread cut into rectangle and toasted on al sides.
Make custard according to the direction on the pack.

PLATING TOOLS NEEDED

Spoon
Pipping bag

INSTRUCTION

1. Divide the beans into three parts for smooth and easing blending.
2. Put the first part in the blender with one egg, some pepper, half of the onion and tatashe with a little water.
3. Blend it into a smooth and thick batter (very important).
4. Pour the batter into a large mixing bowl.
5. Continue the process till everything is done.
6. Fit the bowl in the stand mixer with the whisk attachment or you can use the electric hand mixer or a balloon whisk.
?. Season with salt to taste then whip on medium high speed till it doubles in size or light and airy.
8. Heat the oil in a fry pan over a medium high heat.
g. Add the remaining onion into the oil for flavour.
10. With the use of spoon, scoop the batter nicely into the hot oil and fry till golden brown (once the oil is too hot the Kosai will burn and when the oil is not hot enough the Kosai will soak oil).
11. Drain on paper towel.
12. Serve hot with pap, bread or whatever you fancy.
Note: to make the tuile, add water to the batter to make the consistency a bit thinner and fry.

TO ASSEMBLE

1. Arrange the broken mortar if you have. You can use a Woden chopping board or a tile.
2. Pipe the pap nicely on it.
3. Place one Akara on top and a tuile on the side.
4. Sprinkle some yaji on top.
5. Serve immediately.

TO ASSEMBLE FOR BREAD AND CUSTARD

1. Go crazy with whatever you want to serve i with.
2. Place the toasted bread on it.
3. Fill up the piping bag with custard, use a sharp knife to cut the tip nicely.
4. carefully pipe the custard on the bread.
5. Divide three Kosai into two and place it carefully on top of the custard.
6. Pipe some more custard in between the kosai.

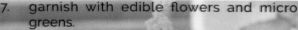

7. garnish with edible flowers and micro greens.
8. Serve immediately.

Danwake
literally Son of Beans!

This is our very own dumpling made out of beans flour, amazing right? I know .. lol! Can be paired with pretty much any sauce but guess what? How we present this is not cool. Let me show you something. Kala!

INGREDIENTS	PLATING TOOLS NEEDED
1 cup danwakeflour(bean flour) 1 free range chicken (local chicken) cut into eight pieces andwashed 1medium onion cleanand slicedthinly 1kg tomatoes washed 7 habaneros or as desiredwashed 3 tatashe deseeded and washed 1tsp curry 1tspthyme 1tspmincedgarlic 1tsp mincedginger 1/2 cup vegetable oil 4 hard boiled egg. peeled and cut into quarters 5 lettuce,cleaned and shredded Salt and seasoning to taste	Spoon Tong **TO ASSEMBLE** 1. Get a nicelooking flatplate. 2. Pick one of the drumstick with the tong and place it close to one side of the plate by slanting it. 3. Use the spoon to scoop the danwake and place on the plate like a zig zag using the chicken as guide. 4. Add the eggsnicely. 5. Someonionthen thelettuce. 6. Use the spoon to scoop some of the sauce and place it carefully on the plate. 7. Serveimmediately.

INSTRUCTION

1. Combine the Tomato , pepper, tatashe in a blender and blendtillsmooth.
2. Pour the mix in a saucepan. place over medium high heat and cook tillcompletely reduced.
3. Place the chicken in another saucepan over a medium highheat.
4. Add the curry. thyme, ginger. garlic, some onion, salt andseasoning to taste.
5. Cover and let steam in its juice for 1ominutes.
6. Add some water, cover and let cook tillfork tender. Take out of heat. pour it in a large bowl and place the pot back on and let the heat dry the remaining liquidinthepot.
7- Pour the oil. add some of the onions reservingjustalittleforgarnish.
8. Fry tilltranslucent. Add the pepper mix and stirto combine.
g. Fry for 10 minutes.Add the chicken and the stock.
10. Stir. reduce the heat to medium low and let

it cook for another 20minutes.
11. Season to taste andset aside.
12. Cook the danwake according to the instructions on the pack.
13. Drain and setaside.

STREET CORNERS

Okpa ...Okpa di Oku!

Highly nutritious. it has won the heart of people from different parts of the country and will win more. Come on and see what we are doing with okpa.

INGREDIENTS	PLATING TOOLS NEEDED
4009 bambara nut flour 1/2 cup palm oil 1 small spring onion blended and green part reserve for garnish 300ml warm beef stock or water 2 tbsp ground dried prawns Salt and seasoning to taste 1 tbsp cayenne pepper or as desired 1 habanero minced	Donut silicon mould

INSTRUCTION

1. Pour the flour in a large bowl.
2. Add the cayenne pepper, ground dried prawns and stir to combine.
3. Add the palm oil. blended onion. minced habanero, the stock or water, seasoning and salt to taste.
4. Stir vigorously into a smooth and thin consistency.
5. Adjust the seasoning. grease the mould and fill halfway.
6. Place a large pot that can take the size of the mould over a medium high heat.
7- Add a little water in the pot and bring to a simmer.
8. Place bits of stick at the bottom of the pot to help with the steaming.
9. Place the mould on top of the sticks in the pot and cover.
10. Let steam for 45 - 1 hour checking occasionally to add water into the pot.
11. Serve hot with custard or pap.

TO ASSEMBLE

1. Get a flat plate of choice.
2. Place two rings of the okpa on a plate.
3. Place the third one top of the first two.
4. Slant the fourth one by the side.
5. Divide the fifth into two and place the half or top of the first okpa and the second half slanted by the side of the other one.
6. Sprinkle pepper sauce on it and garnish with the green part of the spring onion.
7. Serve immediately.

STREET CORNERS

Fried Yam & Pepper Sauce
(Dundun & Ata Dindin)

...street credibility!

Easy to make and even easier to eat. lol. Very simple. delicious. crunchy texture on the outside. a sweet or savoury dish that can be served as an appetiser. a little twist and it will become a main, small shift like this you have a side. It practically brings people together while snacking on this beauty. It saved my life back then in school. Still saving life because of its simplicity. Since happiness is about eating spicy street food with friends. I decided to elevate fried yam from how you know it to be, to something it can be and more...Salute!!!

INGREDIENTS	PLATING TOOLS NEEDED
FOR THE YAM (DUNDUN)	Pairing knife
1 tuber of yam peeled and cut into very thick slices	Spoon
Salt to taste	Tweezer
Vegetable oil for deep frying	
FOR THE PEPPER SAUCE (ATA DINDIN)	**TO ASSEMBLE**
1 cup palm oil	1. Get a plate of your choice make sure it's flat.
3 tatashe cleaned and chopped	2. Use the spoon to scoop the sauce and place it nicely on the plate and swoosh it to the direction you want.
5 habanero or as desired cleaned and chopped	
1 medium ripe tomatoes cleaned and chopped	3. Place the yam in the middle. scoop some of the smooth sauce inside.
1 small onion cleaned and sliced	4. Arrange the flaked fish nicely, garnish with micro greens and some of the rough sauce.
2 tbsp blended dried prawns	
Salt and seasoning to taste	5. Serve immediately.
1 fried mackerel deboned	

INSTRUCTION

FOR THE YAM (DUNDUN)
1. Use the pairing knife to shape the yam into a nice square about 3"high and 3" wide.
2. Create a hollow on top of the yam and scoop out the excesses.
3. You want to have it looking like a box with a hole in the middle.
4. Continue the process till all the slices are exhausted.
5. Put the yam in a pot covered with water and season with salt to taste.
6. Place it over a medium high heat and let simmer for 10mins. drain and set aside.
7. Heat a deep frying pan with oil over a medium high heat till hot.
8. Add the yam and deep fry till golden brown.
9. Drain on paper towel and set aside.

FOR THE SAUCE (ATA DINDIN)
10. Heat the palm oil in a medium saucepan over a medium heat.
11. Add the sliced onion and let fry for 2 minutes or till fragrant.
12. Add the tatashe. habanero pepper and tomato.
13. Reduce the heat to medium low and let it fry for about 10mins stirring occasionally.
14. Add the blended dried prawn and season to taste.
15. Let fry for another 2 minutes and its ready.
16. Take about 3 tablespoons of the rough pepper sauce and set aside.
17. Blend the remaining into a smooth consistency and pass it through a fine sieve to give a smooth and glossy sauce.

Get Your
Soups On

White Soup with Uziza Oil

prominent. spicy, unique, mouth watering and it is elegant. Perfect with pounded yam. White soup is Ah Ma Zing!

INGREDIENTS

1 whole free range chicken (local chicken) washed, pat dry andcut intoquarter (into 4)
1 thick slice of yam, peeled, washed and cut intocubes
1tbspthinly sliceduziza leaf for garnish
2 tbspgroundcrayfish
2medium dry fishwashed and deboned
5yellow habaneros or asdesired blended
2009 stock fishwashed
2 tbspgroundcrayfish
1/ 4 tsp ground uziza
2udaseed
1tspokpei
1smallonion minced
Salt and seasoning to taste

FOR THE UZIZA OIL

1 cup chilledvegetable oil
2cup sliceduziza leaves
Pinch of salt
Bowlof icedwater
Cheesecloth

PLATING TOOLS NEEDED

Ladle
Squeeze bottle

TO ASSEMBLE

1. Get a nice plate, brush the ladle with a little oil.Scoop the morselof choice.
2. Place on the plate. wet the back of the ladle with warm water, sprinkle oil again and use to to createa holein the middle.
3. Fill the hole up with the white soup, place the chicken leg on one end and drizzle uziza oil.
4. Serveimmediately.

INSTRUCTION

1. Heat a large pot over medium highheat.
2. Add the chicken, onionand season to taste.
3. Let the chickencook in it'sjuice tilldry.
4. Add water to cover, bring to a boil andlet cook for 10 minutes.
5. Add the dried fish, stock fish, uda, pepper, yamand cook untilyamis tender.
6. Take out the yam and pound into a smooth pasteusingmortar and pestle.
7. Use a spoon to scoop the yam paste bit bybit intothepot andstirto combine.
8. Add the crayfish, okpei. uziza. Let simmer for 5 minutes or until yam paste is completely dissolved.
9. Add water to adjust consistency if its too thick.
10. Adjust seasoning to taste.
11. Serve hot.

FOR THE UZIZA OIL

1. Bring a pot of water to a boil.
2. Blanch the uziza leaves in the boiling water for about10seconds.
3. Remove quickly with a strainer and dunk in the ice water, swishing themaround tillcold.
4. Remove from water and place on paper towelto drain it.
5. Put the leaves in a blender. add the salt and oilandblendtillsmooth.
6. Place the cheesecloth over a clean bowl. pour over the blended uziza and let it drain. Donut squeeze.
7. Pour the oil into a squeeze bottle. Can be storedfor 8-10 days in the fridge.

Epe Eza ...Rainy Day!

This soup keeps the memory of my grandmother alive in my heart every time. She loved making it with dry fish and uka(amala) mostly when it's raining to keep warm. Hearty meal with great texture. It's made out of beans and it is very popular in Ebira land.... Av6!

INGREDIENTS

1 cup black eyed peas, picked and dry blend coarsely
1 cup palm oil
2 tbsp iru(locust beans)
3 large dry fish cleaned and deboned
5 habanero washed or as desired blended
1 chicken breast cleaned, seasoned and pan seared
2 tbsp ground crayfish
Salt and seasoning to taste
2 litre water
A handful of washed dried bitter leaf or leafy green of choice (optional). I used basil for garnish

PLATING TOOLS NEEDED

Cling film

INSTRUCTION

1. Put the washed fish in a large pot. blended pepper, locust bean, crayfish. salt and seasoning to taste. water and place over a medium high heat.
2. Let it cook till the fish is tender.
3. Add the palm oil and cook for another 3 minutes.
4. Use slotted spoon to scoop out cooked fish into a bowl and set aside.
5. Reduce the heat to low and whisk in the blended beans vigorously to prevent lumps.
6. Return the fish into the soup and let cook over medium heat for 10 -15 minutes.
7. Add the leafy green of choice. adjust seasoning and serve immediately.

TO ASSEMBLE

1. Lay morsel of choice on the cling film.
2. Spread it flat quickly while still very hot.
3. Then fold it like ayoga mat.
4. Use a clean knife to cut the sides off. then slice neatly.
5. Get a nice looking plate.
6. Place the morsel diagonally on the plate.
7. Nicely cut the Chicken breast vertically and place it side by side with the morsel.
8. Add the soup neatly.
9. Garnish with basil.
10. Serve immediately.

GET YOUR SOUPS ON

Okra Soup ...StewedUp!

Deliciously satisfying. nutritious. loaded with healthy fat. If you are not disciplined. this soup willmakeyoueatmorethanyoubargained for .... lol!

INGREDIENTS

500g okra, washed and finely chopped
5 habanero or asdesired finely mined
1 smallonion finely minced
1 tbspground crayfish
2 largedry fish.washed and deboned
1/2 cup palmoil
1 friedwhite fish filledcut intochunks
Salt and seasoning to taste
1 litrewater
1/4 tspground uziza
1/4 tsp ground ehuru

PLATING TOOLS NEEDED

Piping bag
Roundpipping tip

INSTRUCTION

1. Put the dried fishin a large pot.
2. Add the pepper. onion. water. seasoning to taste.
3. Place over medium high heat and cook till fishis tender.
4. Add the palm oil. okra and cook for 3-5 minutes.
5. Add the crayfish. ehuru and uziza powder. Stir to combine.
6. Adjust seasoning andserve.

TO ASSEMBLE

1. Fit the roundpipping tip inthe piping bag.
2. Scoop morselof choice in the pipingbag.
3. Get a nice plate and make like a snail shell by pressing like three to four times on one side of the plate. leaving a smallarea for the soup.
4. Make a mix of smallto medium.
5. Add the soup and place the fish chunks around it.
6. Serveimmediately.

Egusi Soup ..Classic!

This isa clear case of "how you like me now"... like youcan make this soup however you want it andit willstillbegreat. Iknow you get what· 1 m trying to say. Take a goodlook at that!

INGREDIENTS

5009 blended egusi(melon seeds)
1cuppalmoil
1medium onion cleaned
3ripe tatashe cleaned
5ripe tomatoes cleaned
10 habaneros or asdesiredcleaned
2009 stock fishwashed
1 medium croaker cut into steaks, head off. washed seasoned and set aside
5 prawns deveined and cleaned with tailon. seasoned and setaside
3handfulspinach,washed and sliced
Salt and seasoning taste
2tbsp iru(Locust beans)
1tbspground crayfish
1 Litre meat stock

PLATING TOOLS NEEDED

Tong
Spoon
Cling film

INSTRUCTION

1. Combine the tatashe, pepper, onion, tomato. and blend into a smooth paste then set aside.
2. Put the blended egusi in a clean bowl. sprinkleaLittle water and mix intoapaste.
3. Placea Largepot over amedium high heat.
4. Add the oil.sear the fisha bit and set aside.
5. Now drop the egusi paste bit by bit into the oil and give it a quick fry by stirring occasionally.
6. Add the blended tomato mix, stock fish. dry fish,cover and bring toa boil.
7- Let it boilvigorously for 5minutes.
8. Give it a quick stir, add the meat stock, iru. and Let cook for 10 minutes stirring occasionally.
g. Add the fish, crayfish. prawns and cook for another 8 minutes.
10. Adjust seasoning to taste. sprinkle some of the spinach.
11. Serve with morselof choice.

TO ASSEMBLE

1. Get a flatplate that canshow the dish.
2. Lay the cling film on a flatsurface.
3. Scoopout morselof choice.
4. Rollit intoaslimrod.
5. Place on the plate.
6. Wet the back of the spoon and make a hole to form acanoe.
7- Press the edges.
8. Scoop the soup into the hole.
g. Use the tongto arrange the fish and prawns.
10. Sprinkle some of the spinach and serve.

Mackerel. Amala, Gbegiri, Ewedu And Stew ...thetrinity!

This queen right here deserve all the hailings because it's super cool. It breaks my heart when I see how its been presented on a plate with all the beautiful complementary colours without making it look good for people who are not familiar with the dish to even try it. This isa delicacy you do not only find on the streets but at weddings. christening and all. Personally. I feelamala deserves some accolades. It taste glorious but needs that eye catching presentation that will makeyoujust wanna frame it. Here's my interpretationof the dish.

INGREDIENTS

FOR THE GBEGIRI
1009 beans.peeled andwashed
1/2 cup palmoil
3habaneros blended or as desired
2cupstock
1smallonion minced
Seasoning and saltto taste

FOR THE EWEDU
2bunches eweduUute leaves). cleaned and sliced
209 locust beans(iru)
2cupstock
2tbspground crayfish
Salt and seasoning to taste
2largedry fish cleanedand deboned

FOR THE STEW
15 large red tomatoes cleaned
8 tatashe. cleaned anddeseeded
1 medium onion cleaned. sliced and few reserved
6 habaneros or asneeded
2cups palm oil
1kgassorted meat cleaned
1tsp ginger powder
1tsp garlic powder
Salt and seasoning to taste

FORTHEAMALA
2cup yam flour (elubo)
4cupwater
1cuphotwater reserved
1tbspvegetable oil

FOR THE MACKEREL
4mackerel
Salt and seasoning to taste
1cup vegetable oil

PLATINGTOOLS NEEDED
Ring cutter
Piping bag
Smalloffset spatula

GET YOUR SOUPS ON

INSTRUCTION

FORTHESTEW

1. combine the tomato, pepper, tatashe and onion in a blender and blend into a smooth paste.
2. Put the assorted meat in a medium saucepan, add the reserved onion, garlic powder. ginger powder. seasoning. salt to taste, cover with lid and place over a medium highheat.
3. Letsteamfor5minsinit'sjuice.
4. Add enough water to cover and cook tillfork tender.
5. Pour the blended tomato over and continue cooking tillreduced to half.
6. Add the palm oil and continue cooking for about10 minutes stirring occasionally.
7. Reduce heat and let simmer for another 10 minutes.
8. Adjust seasoning and consistency then set aside.

FORTHEGBEGIRI

1. Pour the cleaned beans in a saucepan over a medium high heat. add the minced onion. the stock, and cook tillmushy.
2. Add the palm oil. the blended habaneros, seasoning and cook for another 15 minutes
3. Take it off heat. blend till smooth and creamy using the immersion blender.
4. Adjust seasoning and consistency then set aside.

FOR THE EWEDU

1. Place the ewedu ijute leaves) in a blender with1 cupof thestock and blitz as desired.
2. Pour the remaining stock in asaucepan,add the fish and placeover a medium high heat.
3. Cook tillthefishistender.
4. Addthe crayfish and locust beans (iru).
5. Pour the blended ewedu over and stir to combine.
6. Reduce the heat to medium low and let it cook for 3minutes.
7. Adjust seasoning to taste andsetaside.

FORTHEAMALA

1. Bring the 4 cups of water to boil over medium highheat.
2. Reduce the heat to lowest. add the vegetableoil and theyam flour.
3. Stir with wooden spoon vigorously to combinenicely.
4. You want to get a soft, smooth and pliable dough.
5. Add the reserved water, cover and let it steam for 5 minutes to enable it cook through.
6. Stir vigorously one more time and mould intodesired shape.
7. Serve hot.

FORTHEFISH

1. Place the fishon a cleanchopping board.
2. Use a sharp knife to make an incision behind the pectoral fin of the mackerel. until the knife hitsthe backbone.
3. Run the knife down the side of the backbone. cutting ascloseto it as possible.
4. Using a sweeping motions. cut the fillet away, keeping as close to the backbone as possible and holding the knife parallel to the board, leaving the headandtailintact.
5. Setthe fillet aside.
6. Trim the fish of excess skin and flesh off the bone.
7- Gently wash with cold water. pat dry and season to taste.
8. Heat up a nonstick frying pan over medium highheat.
g. Addthe oil.once pan is smoking hot,add the mackerelto the fryingpan. skinsidedown.
10. Cook for 2-4 minutes. once the skin is crisp and golden, turn it over, remove the pan fromheat.
11. Leave the mackerel to cook in the residual heat.takeit out and place on a paper towel.

TOASSEMBLE

1. Rollout the amala and cut out a circle with the largest ring cutter or you can start with the size you fancy and place the amala on the plate you want to use.
2. Follow it up with the next cutter but you are not cutting it through this time.
3. Skip two sizes and use the one next to it and pierce but not cutting through.
4. With the use of offset spatula, take out the amala in between to create a space for the soup.
5. Continue the process till you get a space for the three soups.
6. Continue till you have created enough space for the soups.
7. Pour the soups in different pipping bags and carefully fill up the circles with the soups.
8. Carefully place the fish on top and serve!

GET YOUR SOUPS ON

Fisherman Soup ...catch of the day!

Spicy warm. aromatic, Flavour burst. colourful. everything fresh and nice. Can be eaten with rice, yam, potatoes, starch, plantain...etc!!I consulted Ariel on this one and voila!!

INGREDIENTS

5 medium lobsters cleaned and shell intact
7 jumbo prawns cleaned
3 large snails cleaned and butterflied
1 cup periwinkles cleaned
1 large tilapia cleaned and cut into steaks
1 tbsp ground crayfish
3-4 fingers okra thinly sliced
1/2 cup palm oil
1/4 tsp ground uziza seeds
5 uziza leaves sliced
5 habaneros or as desired blended
1 small onion cleaned and blended
1 tsp cayenne pepper
1/2 cup pounded cocoyam
Salt and seasoning to taste

PLATING TOOLS NEEDED

Cling film
Ladle

INSTRUCTION

1. Make the pounded cocoyam by boiling a few tubers, peel and pounding using a mortar to form a smooth dough.
2. In a medium size pot. add the snail, the blended pepper, cayenne pepper, onion, seasoning and salt to taste.
3. Place over a medium high heat. add 2 cups of water and boil for 20 minutes.
4. Add the lobster and fish steaks.
5. Boil for for 5 minutes..
6. Add the prawns and cook for another 5 minutes.
7. Carefully take out all the seafood into a bowl, add the cocoyam to thicken the broth by stirring properly to dissolve nicely.
8. Add the ground uziza seed. periwinkles. palm oil and let simmer for about 2 minutes.
g. Return the seafood back into the pot. add the sliced okra. crayfish. sliced uziza leaves. adjust seasoning and let simmer for 2 minutes.
10. Serve hot.

TO ASSEMBLE

1. Get a deep bowl that can still show everything on the plate (not too deep).
2. Use cling film to roll up the starch like a short fat sausage then set aside.
3. Place the lobster nicely on one side of the plate.
4. Then the prawns on the other side.
5. Arrange the snail opened up and placed next to the lobster.
6. Carefully place the starch on the snail.
7- Use the ladle to gently scoop the soup and pour it around nicely.
8. Serve immediately.

GET YOUR SOUPS ON

Eforiro ...Dramatic!

This one would just leave you hanging if you do not thread with caution. So fragile and saucy. Don't ask me about that... lol!

INGREDIENTS

2 bunches of spinach. washed. blanched and sliced
3 red tatashe washed
5 habaneros or as desired washed
1 medium onion cleaned. cut into halves and thinly slice the other
4 ponmo {cow skin} . washed and cut into chunks
4 mackerel. heads off. cleaned. seasoned and deepfry
1 cup palmoil
2 tbsp crayfish
2 tbsp locustbeans
3 large dried fish washed and deboned
Salt and seasoning to taste

PLATING TOOLS NEEDED

Plastic cutter

INSTRUCTION

1. Combine the pepper. the remaining half onion. tatashe and blend coarse then set aside.
2. Heat up the oil in a large pot over a medium heat for about 2 minutes.
3. Add the sliced onion and fry till fragrant.
4. Add the iru. fry for about a minute.
5. Add the blended ingredients . ponmo and dry fish. season to taste and let fry for 15 - 20 minutes.
6. Add the blanched spinach and toss nicely.
7. Adjust seasoning. to taste.
8. *Serve* hot.

TO ASSEMBLE

1. Get a nicelooking plate.
2. Wet the plastic cutter with oily water to scoop morsel of choice.
3. Place on the plate and wet the cutter again.
4. Use it to create lines on it by spreading it as well.
5. Scoop the soup on it. place the ponmo strategically and lay the fish.
6. *Serve* immediately.

Apart from it being a hearty soup with chunks of whatever protein you fancy and other condiments. The **technicality in preparing this soup** is **amazing and it got me asking questions like.... why donl we just** spend that extra seconds to make it look "shazzam", like a magic show. Why are we so impatient with food plating? honestly it is not that hard. This soup is primarily liquid, usually serve hot with basically whateveryou feel comfortable having it with. Made out of broth with robust flavours from our authentic spices, it adds that extra zing to your day iif you are feeling a little bit under the weather. It is royal and absolutelystunning. PermitmetosayECHOKE!!!!

INGREDIENTS

1 medium tilapia or croaker cut into steaks and cleaned

2009 prawns. shells removed, cleaned and deveined

1009 calamaricleaned

8-10 king crab legscleaned

1/2 tsp ehuru powder(calabashnutmeg)

1/4 tsp uzizapowder

2 tbsp minced habaneros or asdesired

1 spring onion minced (whitepart only)

1 tsp minced ginger

1 tsp minced garlic

Juice of half lemon

15scent leaf cleaned and shredded

Salt and seasoning to taste

2 litrewater

PLATING TOOLS NEEDED

Tweezer
Measuringjug
Tong
Cheese cloth

INSTRUCTION

1. Put the fish in a pot. add the ginger, garlic, habaneros, onion, seasoning and salt to taste.
2. Place the pot overamedium low heat. cover tightly and let steam for 5minutes.
3. Add 1 litre of water, increase the heat to medium highand bring tojust aboil.
4. Add the calamari. prawns and let cook for 3 minutes.
5. Add the crab legs, uziza powder, ehuru powder and cover tightly to simmer for 5 minutes.
6. Add the lemonjuice and adjust seasoning.
7. Add the scent leaf and serve hot..

TO ASSEMBLE

1. Get a nice soup bowl.
2. Carefully pick out the seafood with the tong and arrange nicely in the soup bowl by stacking it up.
3. Place the cheese cloth over a measuringjug and scoop out somebroth using the ladle.
4. Pour over the Cheese cloth to collect a clearerbroth.
5. Pour the broth over the nicely arranged seafood. Add enough but do not cover the seafood completely.
6. Use the tweezer to arrange the micro greens.
7. Serveimmediately.

Afang Soup

...the queen!

A delight to behold... to be eaten... to be enjoyed and stylish to appease the eyes.

INGREDIENTS

5009 beefcleanedandcut intochunks
1/2 cup stock fish flakes cleaned
2 medium dry fishcleaned anddeboned
1 cup periwinkle cleaned
8009 cow leg cleaned andcut intochunks
1 bunchesofwaterleafwashedandsliced
5cups Afang leaves pounded
5 yellow pepper (habanero) cleaned and blended
1 cup palmoil
1/2 cup grounded crayfish
Salt andseasoning to taste
2 litrewater

PLATING TOOLS NEEDED

1M decorating tip
Piping bag

INSTRUCTION

1. Place the cow leg in a pressure pot. season to taste.add 1 litre water, cover and let cook it pressurecook for 15minutes.
2. In a large pot. add the beef, season to taste, place over a medium high heat and let steamin its own juicetillalmost dry.
3. Add the pressure cooked cow leg, stock fish. the remaining 1 litre water and cook till soft.
4. Add the pepper.dry fish.crayfish. periwinkle and let boilfor5minutes.
5. Add the palm oil.cook for 3minutes.
6. Add the sliced waterleaf and let cook for 3 minutes.
7- Turn off the heat and add the pounded afang. stirwelltocombine.
8. Servehot with morselof choice.

TO ASSEMBLE

1. Geta plate of choice.
2. Fitthepiping tip in apiping bag.
3. Fillit upwithmorselof choice.I usedeba.
4. Pipe it on one side of the plate leaving enough spacefor the soup.
5. Addthe soupcarefully.
6. Serve immediately.

Jollof Rice

.the key to Happiness! (Belle the sweet me!)

This rich, incredibly tasty (especially when it's smoky), one pot dish is so amazing that you can never get enough of it. this dish will just be screaming "eat me eat me" literally. It's in a class of its own, "them no dey follow Jollof drag". This dish is made from a rich tomato sauce, great stock and most importantly top quality grain of rice. If a dish can make life easy for you, why can't you appreciate it in return by making it more gorgeous? This dish is a party pleaser and if you ask me. deserves all the ACCOLADES. Chin chin!!!

INGREDIENTS

4 cups rice washed and parboiled for 10 mins
8 large tatashe deseeded and cleaned
4 large very ripe tomatoes
3 habaneros or as desired
3 cups beef/lamb stock
1 medium onion cleaned and sliced
100g tomato paste
112 cup vegetable oil
2 tsp minced ginger
112 tsp curry powder
112 tsp thyme
2 bay leaf
Salt and seasoning to taste

FOR THE LAMBSHANK

5 Lambshank cleaned
1 small onion thinly sliced
1 tsp curry powder
1 tsp dried thyme
1/4 tsp freshly grated nutmeg
2 habaneros cleaned and cut into halves
1/2 tsp oregano
1 tsp ginger powder
1 tsp garlic power
1 tsp paprika
1/2 tsp cayenne pepper
Vegetable oil for frying

FOR THE PLANTAIN

3 fingers plantain washed and peeled
Salt to taste
vegetable oil for frying

PLATING TOOLS NEEDED

Ring mould
Spoon

INSTRUCTION

FOR THE SHANK

1. Place the shank in a medium pot.
2. Add all the herbs and spices.
3. Season to taste.
4. Cover tightly, place over a medium low heat and let steam for 5-10 mins.
5. Open and add 1 litre water. cover and let cook tiLL tender.
6. Strain and set the stock aside for later use.
7. Heat the Vegetable oil in a deep frying pan and let hot.
8. Fry till golden brown and drain on paper towel.
9. Set aside for later use.

FOR THE PLANTAIN

1. Slice the peeled plantain lengthwise and season with salt to taste
2. Heat up the oil in a deep frying pan over medium high heat.
3. Deep fry till golden brown and drain on a paper towel. Set aside for later.

FOR THE JOLLOF RICE

1. Combine the tomatoes, pepper, half of the sliced onions. tatashe in a blender and blend till smooth.
2. Pour the mix in a medium sauce pan and place over a medium high heat.
3. Cook and stir occasionally till the liquid is completely reduced.
4. Pour the mix in a bowl and set aside.
5. In a medium pot over medium low heat. add the vegetable oil, the remaining onion, thyme, bay leaf, and let fry till fragrant.
6. Add the tomato paste, the reduced tomato, garlic. ginger, curry powder and continue frying till it caramelises about 10 min or when the sauce looks grainy and the colour looks deeper.

7. Scoop a little and reserve for plating later.
8. Stir in rice and stir till welll combined and coated with the sauce. Add the beef stock, cover with a tight fitting lid, increase the heat to medium high. then bring to a boil.
9. Let it boil vigorously for about 10 mins.
10. Reduce the heat to medium low and let it steam so the rice can soak up the richness of the sauce. About 10 to 15 minutes.
11. Open the lid and check for the doneness of the rice. Season to taste,.
12. Once the rice is cooked. turn up the heat with the lid on and leave to "burn" for 3 to 5 minutes. You'll hear the rice crackle and snap and it willl smell toasted.
13. Turn off the heat and leave with the lid on to "rest" till ready to serve. The longer the lid stays on, the smokier the taste. (you can skip 12 and 13 if you don't want it smoky).
14. Serve hot with plantain and protein of choice.

TO ASSEMBLE

1. Get a suitable plate i.e (a round white plate).
2. Place the ring mould in the centre of the plate.
3. carefully scoop the rice with a spoon into the mould and press tightly.
4. Once you get halfway. place the meat nicely, fold the plantain gently and place it close to the meat.
5. Add more rice and press to hold the meat and plantain into position.
6. Once that is completed, carefully remove the ring mould.
7. Place one bay leaf nicely in the middle and add some of the sauce nicely on it.
8. Serve immediately.

Fried Rice.. Colour Me!

Nigerian fried rice likes to be pretty all the time. This dish is a Diva!

INGREDIENTS

2 cups longgrain rice washed and parboiled
1 kg chicken wings cleaned and cut into drumette and wingette
1/2cupfrozen peas
2 carrots peeled and finely diced
1/4 cup sweet corn
2 tsp curry
2tspthyme
1/4 cup finely diced red bellpepper
1/4 cup finely diced green bellpepper
1habanero or as desired minced
1 spring onion minced and green part finely sliced
2tsp minced ginger
2tsp minced garlic
Salt and seasoning to taste
Vegetable oil for frying
1cup barbecue sauce

FOR THE COLESLAW

1/4 red cabbage head washed and finely sliced
1/4 white cabbage head washed and finely sliced
1 large carrot washed, peeled and finely shredded
2 lettuce leaves, washed and finely shredded
1/4 cup Mayonnaise
Juice of half lemon
1 tbsp water
1tbsp of sugarorhoney

PLATING TOOLS NEEDED

Rectangularmould
Squeeze bottle

INSTRUCTION

1. Place the chickenwing ina pot.
2. Add 1 tsp each curry,thyme, ginger,garlic and season to taste.
3, Let steam in its liquid for 5 minutes over a medium highheat. then add 1 litre water.
4. Let cook for 10 minutes, drain strain and set asideto cool.
5, Pour the chicken stock in a pot. and the remaining curryand bring to a boil.
6. Add the rice in the stock and cook tilldesired doneness.Set aside to cool.
7- Pour enough oil in a deep frying pan till hot overamedium high heat.
8. Deep fry the chicken wings tillgolden brown, drain intoa bowl,toss it in barbecue sauce and set aside.
g. Place a wok over a medium high heat. add 1/4 cup of the oil used in frying the chicken.
10. Add the cooked rice,peas, carrots and tossed using wooded spoon.
11. Add the bell peppers,green part of the onion and season to taste.
12. Turnoff heat and set aside.
13. Make the dressing for the slaw by mixing the mayo,honey,lemonjuice and water.
14. Mix vigorously to combine.
15. Pourinto a squeeze bottle and set aside.
16. Toss the red and white cabbage, carrot and lettuce together ina cleanbowland set aside.

TO ASSEMBLE

1. Get anice looking place.
2. Make nice drizzles with your mayonnaise on the plate.
3, Scoop the rice into the rectangular mould and press tightly.
4, Place the plate on top of the mould and turn it over.
5, Remove the mould.
6. Place two chicken drumettes in between the moulded rice.
7, Use spoon to scoop the slaw and place it around the plate.
8. Serve immediately.

PARTY STARS

Moi Moi with Meaty Sauce & Egg

...Soft Life!

Very common at parties, can be prepared and eaten in different ways. People pleaser, soft and smooth texture. You just have to love this soft queen!

INGREDIENTS

2 cups peeled beans soaked in water for at least 30 minutes
1 small onion
3 habaneros or as desired
2 large tomatoes washed
4 red tatashe deseeded and washed
3 hard boiled eggs
1 cup beef stock
3 tbsp ground dried prawns
Salt and seasoning to taste
3/4 cup vegetable oil

FOR THE MEATY SAUCE

2 tbsp vegetable oil

INSTRUCTION

1. Pour 1 litre of water in a large pot over medium high heat.
2. In a blender. combine the soaked beans, onion. tatashe. tomatoes. habanero and 1 cup of the stock.
3. Blend into a smooth paste.
4. Empty the mix into a large bowl and whisk for about 3 minute.
5. Add the oil. ground dried prawns. salt and seasoning to taste, whisk to combine properly
6. Pour the remaining stock into the blend. cover and shake gently.
7. Add it into the mixture in the bowl.
8. continue whisking about 2 minutes.
9. Adjust seasoning to taste.
10. Brush the mould with oil. ladle some of the mix into the moulds and fill it up to 3/4 and place in the pot of boiling water.
11. Do not let the water get so high up the mould.
12. Place foil on top to trap the steam, cover tightly.
13. Steam for 35-40 minutes.
14. Serve hot or as desired.

1 medium onion minced
500g minced meat
2 garlic cloves minced
8 -10 ripe tomatoes washed, and blended.
2 tbsp tomato paste
3 habanero minced
Salt and seasoning to taste
1 tsp curry
1 tsp thyme

PLATING TOOLS NEEDED

Bucket shape mould

FOR THE MEATY SAUCE

1. Add the oil. onion to a pot. over medium high heat and saute for 4 minutes.
2. Add the garlic. habanero, curry and thyme. Cook for another 2 minute.
3. Add the minced meat. using your spoon to break it as you go until brown (about 8-10 minute).
4. Stir in the tomatoes. the paste seasoning to taste and bring to a boil.
5. Reduce the heat and let it cook slowly for 30 minutes.
6. Stir occasionally and adjust heat to maintain a simmer for another 5 minutes.
7. Adjust seasoning and serve with moi moi or whatever you fancy.

TO ASSEMBLE

1. Remove the moi moi from the mould and place it on a nice plate.
2. Use your spoon to cut out the size of an egg on the moimoi.
3. Cut the egg into desired shape and place it on the moimoi.
4. Spoon the meat sauce and place it nicely on top the moi moi and around the egg.
5. Garnish with spring onion and parsley.
6. Serve immediately.

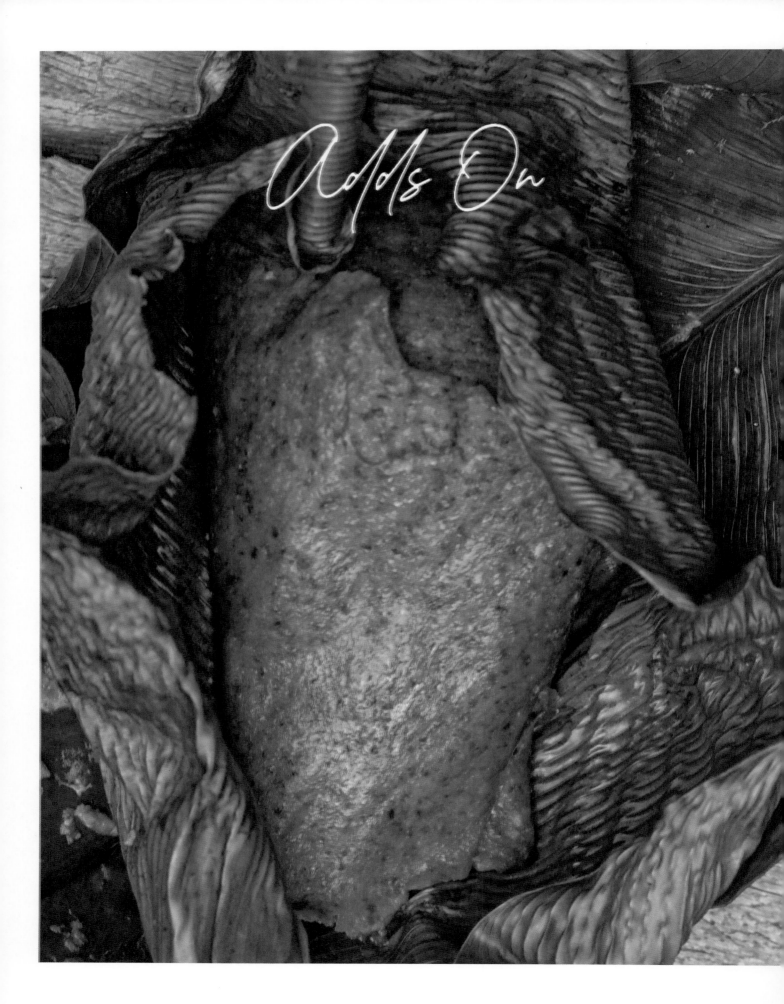

Adds On

ADDS ON

Apapa ...ohiku!

The traditional food of the ebira people of Kogi State. This is very popular most especially during the festive period. Quite feeling, amazing texture, great flavour and of course it is made with my favourite... beans. If you google this food you will be heartbroken because the presentation is bad. Come let me show you how its done...anyase!

INGREDIENTS

4 cup beans (black eyed peas) picked, washed and soaked for at least 30 minutes with the skin on
2 cup palm oil
1 medium onion
3 ripe tatashe
5 habaneros or as desired
2 tbsp ground crayfish
Salt and seasoning to taste
1 tsp edible potash dissolved in 1/4 cup water
1-2 cup water
Moi moi leaf (uma leaf) washed

PLATING TOOLS NEEDED

Noon

INSTRUCTION

1. Put the beans with the pepper, onion. tatashe, with a little water and blend into a rough paste (you don't want it smooth).
2. Pour out the blended beans into a bowl.
3. Add the palm oil and mix vigorously using a whisk.
4. Add the crayfish and season to taste.
5. Add the dissolved potash, a Little bit of water, adjust seasoning to taste and mix to combine nicely (it should be a drop consistency. not too thick or thin).
6. Place a large pot on the fire with little water and a lot of sticks at the bottom of the pot to aid steaming or you can use a steamer if you have one.
?. Now take the leaf, remove the stalk carefully. roll the part with the stalk into a cone and bend the pointed end inwards and hold it with your hand.
8. Scoop the beans mixture into the leaf. then wrap the opened top and fold it under to secure the mix nicely.

g. Place the wrap on top of the sticks in the pot
10. continue the process till the batter is done.
11. Place some of the Leaves on top to enhance the steaming process.
12. Cover tightly and Let steam for 45mins to 1hr, adding water occasionally to prevent burning.
13. Serve hot.

ADDS ON

Paten Acha   Fit Fam!

Highly nutritious. unique taste. rich. made out of the amazing fonio. I don't even want to talk about the Presentation online. Come with me and see beauty!

INGREDIENTS

1/2 cup fonio(acha) washed
5009 meaty bones cleaned
2 large dry fish cleaned
1 medium spring onion chopped and ((the green part julienned and soaked in cold

water)

1 tbsp ground crayfish
1 medium carrot cut into small dice and ((a few shavings with peeler soaked in cold water)
3 habaneros or as desired
1 large tomato chopped
3 garden eggs chopped

1 dadawa pounded
Few sorrel leaves washed and finely sliced
A handful of spinach washed and finely sliced
Salt and seasoning to taste

1/4 cup roughly chopped toasted

groundnut and 1 tbsp reserved for garnish

PLATING TOOLS NEEDED

Ladle

INSTRUCTION

1. Put the washed meaty bones in a large pot over a medium high heat.
2. Add some chopped onions and season to taste.
3. Cover and let cook in its juice for 5 minutes.
4. Add enough water to cover and cook till tender.

5. Add the blended pepper, dried fish, chopped tomatoes, water to cover and the remaining onions.
6. Cook for another 5 minutes.
7- Add the washed fonio and stir well to combine.
8. Add the cray fish, garden egg, dadawa, chopped carrots let simmer for 2 minutes.
g. Add the sorrel leaves and spinach.
10. Add a little bit of water if its too thick.
11. Add the groundnut and adjust seasoning to taste.
12. Serve hot.

TO ASSEMBLE

1. Get a deep plate.
2. Use the ladle to scoop the pate.
3. Pour it nicely into the plate.
4. Place some meaty bones on it.
5. Strain the vegetables from cold water, pat dry and garnish the pate nicely.
6. Serve immmediately.

ADDS ON

Danderu   pull me in!

Our very own Melt In Your Mouth meat. never knew we have something so gracious tillChef Boxiy introduced me to it and my palatenever remain the same ever since. Wowzas!!!

INGREDIENTS

1 leg of lamb. cleaned. pat dry and cut into three chunks
1/ 4cup groundnut oil
1largeonion cleanedand slicedthinly
1tbspcurry powder
1tbspthyme
1tbspyaji
3inch ginger root peeledandwashed
3 garlic cloves
5habanero cleanedandhalved
1tbspdark soysauce
1tbsp paprika
Salt and seasoning to taste

PLATING TOOLS NEEDED

Noon

INSTRUCTION

1. Combine the onion, pepper, curry, thyme, yaji, ginger, garlic, dark soy, oil. paprika.
2. Roughlyblendandsetaside.
3. Preheat the oven at150 degrees Celsius.
4. Get about 4 sheets of foil paper, layering themon top of each other.
5. Place the meet inalargebowlandseason to taste.
6. Addthe blendedmixand massage well.
7- Gently pour it on the foilandcover tightly till allthesheets areexhausted.
8. Place in the Middle of the oven and slow cook for 8 hours or tillthemeet is falling off thebone.
g. Remove and serve withwhatever you fancy.

TO ASSEMBLE

1. Getanicelooking plate.
2. Arrange sinasir, masa or whatever you want to eat the denderu with in the centre of the plate.
3. Use fork to pullthemeat and mix it with the jus.
4. Scoopsome on the sinasir.
5. Drizzle the jus on top and garnish with green onion.
6. Serveimmediately.

Dambun Shinkafa   got me riced out!

Do you know that this dish is made from broken rice "grits"? Are you aware that you can manipulate this dish to make it vibrant and colourful? Do you know that dambun shinkafa is an alternative to your everyday rice dish? well here you go!

INGREDIENTS

2 cups rice grits (broken rice). washed and soaked in water for 10 minutes
1 small radish cleaned and finely diced
1 red bell pepper cleaned and finely diced

1 green bell pepper cleaned and finely diced

1 medium carrot cleaned and finely diced
1009 pulled meat chopped
1/3 cup toasted groundnut roughly chopped
1/2 cup vegetable oil

A handful of micro radish cleaned and pat dry
Salt and seasoning to taste
1 tbsp yaji or as desired

1 small onion sliced

LATING TOOLS NEEDED

Small ring cutter
Spoon

INSTRUCTION

1. Put water in the bottom of a double boiler up to the water line as marked, place over a medium heat and bring to a boil.
2. Place the steamer on top of the bottom of the double boiler.
3. Pour the soak rice in a heat proof bowl. sprinkle half cup of water on the rice.
4. Place the bowl inside the steamer. cover tightly and let steam for 30 minutes.
5. Take out the rice after 30 minutes, season to taste. fluff with a fork and return back to the steamer and steam for another 45 minutes.
6. In a separate saucepan, pour the vegetable oil and place over a medium low heat till hot.
7- Add the onion, let it fry and infuse into the oil. about 5mins.
8. Tip over the oil in a bowl and set aside.
g. Return the pan back on the heat and saute the chopped peppers and carrot each quickly with seasoning and yaji to taste then set aside.
10. Remove the rice from the steamer, drizzle some of the onion oil. adjust seasoning then. fluff with fork and set aside. (You can steam

the rice for another 20 minutes if you want it to be very soft and sticky).

TO ASSEMBLE

1. Get a plate of your choice. preferably a flat one that can show the colours and elements.
2. Place the ring cutter in the centre.
3. Arrange few of the micro greens around the cutter.
4- With the use of a spoon. scoop some of the rice and start arranging it by slanting it on the plate. (It should be wavy like the blades in a standing fan).
5. Up next is the meat. followed by the carrot. green bell pepper. rice again. groundnut. the meat. red bell peppers till all the ingredients are exhausted.
6. Now remove the ring cutter from the middle and carefully arrange the chopped reddish.
7. rearrange the micro greens by selecting a few and placing it on top of the existing one.
8. Drizzle some of the oil and sprinkle some of the yaji on top.
g. Serve immediately.

Get in the know

- **Amala** - Traditional Nigerian meal made out of yam and/ or cassava or unripe plantain flour
- **Ewedu** - Jute leaves, slightly long edges, flavourful and tender.
- **Asun** - Smoked or roast goat in hot and spicy sauce
- **Ehuru** - Calabash nutmeg or African nutmeg. It is an aromatic, spicy, warm used for flavouring food
- **Uziza seed** - Piper guineese or Ashanti pepper, earthy, pungent spice. It adds distinct warm flavour to food
- **Uda** - Negro pepper an aromatic spice used for flavouring food
- **Habanero** - Atarodo, a hot variety of chilli
- **Stock** - Flavourful liquid obtained from simmering meat and vegetables with aromatic herbs and spices in water. It is used instead of plain water in cooking
- **Iru** - Une, dadawa, Ogiri, locust beans fermented seeds, umami -rich used for flavouring food
- **Tatashe** - Red bell peppers used for soups, sauces, etc
- **Soak** - Make or allow something to become thoroughly wet by immersing it in liquid
- **Blend** - To mix together thoroughly that the things become inseparable
- **Blanch** - To cook an item briefly in boiling water or hot fat before finishing or storing it
- **Steam** - To cook items in vapour bath created by boiling water or other liquids
- **Baste** - To moisten food during cooking with pan drippings, sauce or other liquid
- **Eza** - Beans in Ebira language
- **Apapa** - Traditional Ebira food made out coarsely blended beans
- **Ugba** - Oil bean
- **Jus** - literally "juice" refers to fruit, vegetable and meat juices
- **Whip / Whisk** - To incorporate air
- **Fold** - To carefully combine two mixtures
- **Seasoning** - Adding an ingredient to give foods a particular flavour using salt, pepper, herbs, spices and/or condiments .
- **Abacha** - Cassava shavings
- **Denderu** - Slow cooked meat
- **Sinasir** - Rice pancake
- **Julienne** - Vegetables or other items cut into thin strips
- **Gurasa** - Flat bread

Nigerian Food Plating Series showcases the brilliant talent of Tahir Muneera (Chef Muse). Her passion for food plating and styling is infectious and her ability to transform Nigerian dishes into pure art is celebrated within the covers of this beautiful book.

ABOUT THE AUTHOR

Chef Muse is a professional chef, chef instructor, food stylist and culinary consultant. She has been in the culinary industry for 6 years. Her journey started after she lost her place in the second round of the Knorr Taste Quest cooking show in 2015. She then decided to officially kickstart her culinary journey at Red Dish Chronicles Culinary School in Abuja. After taking the professional course for 6 months, she graduated top of her class and this eventually led to her becoming a chef instructor at the same culinary school.

Chef Muse hosted a masterclass at the GTBANK food and drinks festival in 2018. She has also worked with top brands like Cocacola, Maggi, Dangote, Onga and other reputable brands. Her Mantra "my craft my life" is evident in the multiple eye-catching content she shares with her audience daily on the internet. From popular Nigerian meals to continental meals, Chef Muse is the Muse that keeps giving the culinary industry a special source of artistic inspiration.

ISBN: 978-978-999-624-7

🔲 Chef_muse

Cover Design &
Published by:  dowins driving value to you
www.dowins.ng

Printed in Great Britain
by Amazon